40 Days with

The Acts of the Apostles, Vol. 1

A 40-Day Biblical
Devotional Journal:
Study • Reflect • Discern • Pray

40 Days With… The Acts of the Apostles, Vol. 1
A 40-Day Biblical Devotional Journal: Study Reflect Discern Pray

Common English Bible © 2011. Used by permission. All rights reserved.

ISBN: 978-1717579263

Printed in the United States

Book Design: Velin@Perseus-Design.com

Cover photo credits: magagraphics / Depositphotos.com

PREFACE

As a pastor, I am a big fan of daily devotions. Dedicated time reflecting on Scripture helps me grow in my faith and often helps me keep my daily life in a proper perspective. I have used many different devotionals through the years. This series of devotionals was developed in an attempt to address a few shortcomings I have encountered in devotionals currently available.

- Many devotionals are 365 days. Sometimes, I simply cannot or do not want to make a 365 day commitment to one devotional. Sometimes I want or need to focus my devotion time in another direction for a season – for example, maybe I want to use an Advent devotional. Sometimes, I fall behind a few days and then it becomes a chore to catch up, or I skip the missed days and might lose some of the intended devotional continuity.

- Many devotionals offer a scripture accompanied by the thoughts and relevant stories of the author. While these are frequently insightful and inspirational, the author's voice is primary. My attention drifts away too easily from the Scripture to the author's thoughts and stories. I want a devotional that keeps the Scripture primary and helps me create space for God to talk to me through the Scripture of the day. I want to listen for what God is saying to me…today…in this Scripture.

- Many devotionals jump around from one favorite scripture to the next. Again, these individual daily devotionals may be inspiring and helpful. However, encountering these scriptures out of context may make it difficult to see the "big picture" of the story of God. I want a devotional that allows me to encounter the Scripture within the larger context in which it is found. When you complete a **40 Days With…** devotional, you will gain a familiarity with the subject of that volume.

Additionally, I want to intentionally reflect on what I'm learning and discerning from my daily encounter with Scripture. For these reasons, my **40 Days With…** devotionals will be both devotional and journal. My hope is that you will find this hybrid approach to devotionals to be a helpful resource in your spiritual life. Every 40 days you can immerse yourself in a fresh scriptural devotional.

About the Editor

Rev. Chris Barbieri is an ordained Deacon in the United Methodist Church living in Georgia and serving in the North Georgia Conference. Chris is a recognized leader in the area of adult spiritual formation and church leadership. He serves through Digital Deacon Ministries, LLC as an author and consultant. He enjoys leading studies and small groups and his signature workshop is "Better Bible Teaching Starts Now!" Chris also serves on various leadership boards in his community.

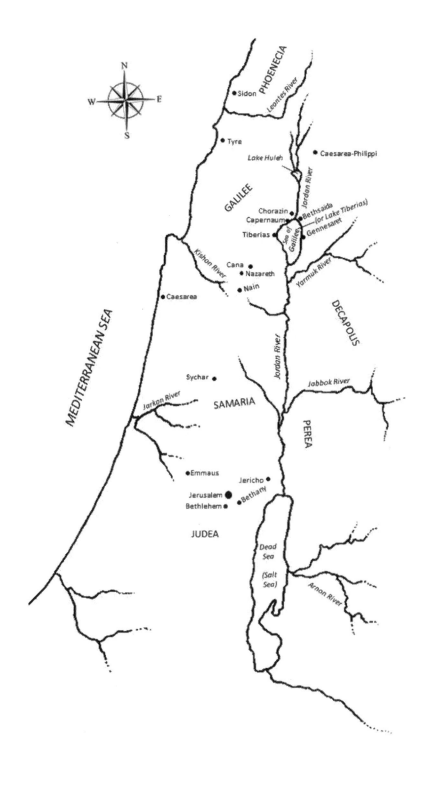

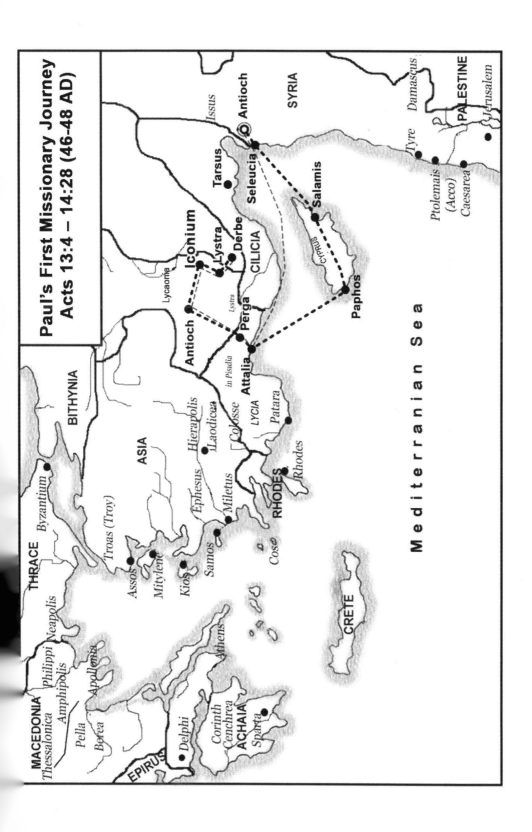

Paul's First Missionary Journey
Acts 13:4 – 14:28 (46-48 AD)

How to use this Devotional

Lectio Divina is an ancient practice of the church in which Christians "prayed the scriptures." Individually or in small groups, a passage of scripture was read three or four times – with silence in between each reading. We should remember that very few people could read in the early church and most people encountered scripture by hearing it. Participants listened carefully, not so they could "learn" in an academic sense. Rather, they listened for how God might be speaking to them in that moment. The ***40 Days With...*** devotionals are designed such that you might listen for God's voice in each day's message in a similar manner.

Know that you will likely get what you put into these devotionals. If you hurry through the reading so you can check it off your to-do list, do not expect many insights or spiritual growth.

As with all devotionals, first find a quiet place free of any distractions. Ideally, you will have a regular place for your devotional time. Plan on spending 15-30 minutes on the devotional pages for the day.

1) Pray – Ask God to clear your mind of the mental clutter and invite the Holy Spirit to speak to you.

2) Turn to your current day's devotional pages.

3) Read the passage slowly and carefully.

4) If possible, read it aloud to yourself a second time.

5) First ask yourself if any words or phrases stand out to you. Don't worry about making sense of them. Simply note these words. Each page has a designated space for you to note these words and phrases.

6) Read the passage again (either silently or aloud, as you prefer.)

7) Reflect on the passage in silence. Do you have any insights? How does this passage apply to you...today? Has this passage put something on your "radar?" Has an image popped in your head as you've reflected? Did this passage raise a question in your mind? Do you particularly identify with anyone in the passage? What emotions are present in the passage? What emotions do you feel as you read the passage?

8) Take 5-10 minutes to write down any thoughts you have had during your time of reflection. Each passage has blank space to record your insights, thoughts, and questions.

9) Read the passage one last time. In this final reading, ask yourself if you feel God calling you to any particular action. Record any additional thoughts you may have.

10) Turn back to the front of the devotional and find the index pages. Find the entry for today's passage. In the "Key Phrase" box, write down the main phrase that you focused on from today's passage. In the "Key Insight" box, try to summarize your thoughts on the passage in one or two sentences.

The first few pages of each devotional volume will serve as an index. You will complete the day's index entry AFTER you have completed the daily devotional pages. In the future, the index may help you reference your insights on a particular passage. You may find it beneficial to periodically review the index pages of a completed devotional.

Know that the Bible is more of a library than a single book. It contains many different books by many different authors. Even within the books, different kinds of scripture are encountered. The Gospels contain a mixture of narrative, teaching, and miracle episodes. The Psalms are poetry and Paul's writings are letters.

The narrative sections may not seem as inspiring as one of Jesus' parables, but these sections are important. They connect the story and help us see where Jesus is and to whom he his is speaking. One of the goals of these devotionals is to help you increase your familiarity with your Bible.

On some days you may be overwhelmed with insights about something Jesus taught. You may feel you need more space to write than the devotional provides. On another day, the scripture may tell the story of Jesus moving from point A to point B and you may not discern any major insights. However, knowing that Jesus moved from A to B might inform the next day's reading. Do not worry about how much or little you hear or write on each day. Simply embrace the process of this daily immersion in Scripture.

WHY THE COMMON ENGLISH BIBLE TRANSLATION WAS CHOSEN

The Common English Bible (CEB) is the most recent English language scholarly translation of the Bible and was published in 2011. The CEB was a cooperative project involving the Disciples of Christ, Presbyterian Church USA, Episcopal Church, United Church of Christ, and United Methodist Church. Several leading Catholic scholars also participated in this project.

An explicit aim of this project was to produce an easily readable English translation. The editors struck a balance between faithful translation of the original ancient texts and readability.

The CEB is a translation, meaning it originates from ancient texts in their original languages. Many "modern" English Bibles are paraphrases in which the editors may or may not take a good deal of interpretive license in translating passages. While paraphrase Bibles can be useful, I have intentionally chosen an English translation which faithfully adhered to strict standards in translating the original Biblical texts.

I have chosen the CEB because:

1) It is the most current translation. I personally know some of the translation editors who worked on this project and I know it was well done.

2) As the newest English translation, many readers will not be familiar with it. Readers are likely to slow down and pay closer attention as they read the CEB. When we slow down and focus on the Scriptures, we make more room for the Holy Spirit to speak us. My hope is that this relatively fresh translation will let you experience the Bible in a fresh way.

Feel free to use another translation if you would like. For ease of use, I wanted to have everything you needed for quality devotional time in one volume. One of the barriers in my own devotional life is I get frustrated when I'm trying to hold a devotional journal steady, balance a Bible (or smartphone/tablet with a Bible app), and try to write something legible. These devotionals are designed such that all you need is a pen and a quiet place.

More on
Translating the Bible

Translating ancient Greek, Hebrew, and Aramaic is not always a straight-forward matter. Some passages are notoriously difficult to translate. Also, our modern Bible did not originate as a "single scroll" that was passed down through the centuries. Rather, there are dozens and dozens of scrolls, fragments, and manuscripts that have come down to us through history. These scrolls do not always agree with one another. Determining which version of a passage is most likely the "original" is a challenging scholarly exercise. Early English translators were not aware of many of these challenging translation issues, resulting in noticeable differences in some passages.

For example, there is a "short ending" and a "long ending" to the book of Mark. Most modern scholars agree that the long ending (verses 9-20) was added in the second century. Any good study Bible will point out these finer points of translation in a footnote.

In the CEB, you will occasionally notice a break in sequence between verse numbers. Most of the time, these breaks mean the translation editors believe the missing verses were not a part of the original Biblical text.

USING THIS DEVOTIONAL AS A SMALL GROUP RESOURCE

In addition to using this devotional as a personal study resource, you may wish to use it in a small group setting. You will find it easy to adapt *40 Days with…* books for use as a 6-week resource in a small group. (Your last week will only have 5 days of material.) Two possible formats for this are offered below. Feel free to develop your own format that fits your setting.

Option 1

1) Agree with all study participants on a common start date and ensure everyone has a copy of the devotional.

2) Meet weekly at an agreed upon time and place for 1 hour to 1 hour and 30 minutes.

3) Identify a facilitator and a prayer leader for each week. The prayer leader will open and close the group with prayer. The facilitator will read the scripture and the guiding questions. So that different voices are part of the experience, the facilitator and prayer leader will not be the same person any given week. You may choose to

rotate responsibilities in your group or have one person designated for each role for your small group.

4) You may wish to use this as a template for your sessions:

- Welcome and opening prayer (5 minutes)

- Spend 5-10 minutes on the prior 6 days' of devotional scripture readings. For each, the facilitator should first ask what words or phrases did people note. Then ask if anyone felt called to any particular action or has an insight to share. If anyone felt called to an action, you may wish to ask the person if he/she would like the group to hold him/her accountable. If so, note this and be sure to ask the person about the action in following weeks. (5 minutes per scripture = 30 minutes, 10 minutes per scripture = 60 minutes)

- Spend 20 minutes experiencing the current day's scripture in *Lectio Divina* style.

  □ Begin with 30 seconds of silence for everyone to clear their minds.

  □ The facilitator should read the scripture. Then allow 30 seconds of silence.

  □ Facilitator say: "Hear the scripture again. Listen for words or phrases that catch your attention." Read the scripture again. Allow 30 seconds of silence. Ask participants to note any key words or phrases in the journal section of the book.

  □ Facilitator invites everyone to close their eyes and hear the scripture a third time. Read the scripture again. Allow 15 seconds of silence. Pause 15-20 seconds between each question below.

1. Ask: What emotions are present in the passage?

2. Ask: Did you identify with anyone in particular in the passage?

3. Ask: Did you feel any particular emotions as you heard the passage?

4. Ask: Has an image popped into your mind as you heard the passage?

5. Ask: How does this passage apply to you…today?

- Invite participants to take a few minutes to record their thoughts in the journal.

- Facilitator say: "Hear the scripture one last time. Do you feel God calling you to some specific action in this passage?" Read the scripture again. Invite people to record any final thoughts.

- Take prayer requests and offer closing prayer (10-15 minutes)

- [Note: You may wish to preview each week's scripture and pre-select one for this *Lectio Divina* experience. It's possible that the group might find one day's scripture more 'interesting' than the seventh day scripture. If you opt for this, be sure to communicate this plan to everyone in your group.]

Option 2

1) Agree with all study participants on a common start date and ensure everyone has a copy of the devotional.

2) Meet weekly at an agreed upon time and place for 1 hour 30 minutes.

3) Rotate responsibility for opening and closing the group with prayer. Use a signup sheet if you wish or simply share the responsibility informally.

4) You may wish to use this as a template for your sessions:

- Welcome and opening prayer (5 minutes)

- Spend approximately 10 minutes on the prior seven days' of devotional scripture readings. For each, the facilitator should first ask what words or phrases did people note. Then ask if anyone felt called to any particular action or has an insight to share. If anyone felt called to an action, you may wish to ask the person if he/she would like the group to hold him/her accountable. If so, note this and be sure to ask the person about the action in following weeks. (10 minutes per scripture = 70 minutes)

- Take prayer requests and offer closing prayer (10-15 minutes)

INTRODUCTION TO THE ACTS OF THE APOSTLES

The Acts of the Apostles (commonly called Acts) is the story of the early church after Jesus ascends to heaven. Acts was written by Luke and continues the story begun in the Gospel of Luke. While Peter and Paul are prominent in Acts, the Holy Spirit is really the main character. Virtually everything of note that occurs, happens through the Spirit. Perhaps a better title for the book would be 'Acts of the Holy Spirit through some of the Apostles."

The Spirit anoints the Disciples at Pentecost, which is sometimes called the "birthday" of the Church. Through the power of the Holy Spirit, both Peter and Paul mirror Jesus' ministry. People are healed and even the dead are raised.

Acts begins with the Disciples, now called Apostles, spreading the good news of Jesus Christ. Peter and John are initially in the spotlight and quickly face persecution from the Jewish leaders. Many early believers scatter throughout Palestine due to this persecution, which only serves to spread the story of Christ. The leaders of the early church face and overcome numerous challenges.

Saul is a passionate persecutor of these early Christians until he encounters the risen Christ on the road to Damascus. Convicted of his error and converted to Christianity, Saul becomes Paul and transforms into a powerful evangelist of the good news. Paul undertakes several long journeys and starts churches throughout Asia Minor and Greece. Paul's zeal for the Gospel angers the Jewish leadership, who make several attempts to kill him. In the end Paul is arrested by the Romans and the legal proceedings ultimately send him to Rome for an appeal to Caesar.

One important aspect of Acts is the expansion of the early church to include Gentiles. This expansion is a controversial issue in the early church, resulting in conflict. However, the church leaders work through this issue and Gentile believers are celebrated and welcomed.

Speeches are a prominent feature of Acts, comprising between 20-30 percent of the book. Peter, Stephen, and Paul make lengthy speeches in Acts. These often start with a retelling of the history of the Israelites and illustrate how Jesus is the fulfillment of Old Testament prophecies. Verses from the Old Testament are regularly cited and each speaker confirms Jesus as Messiah. One could argue that these speeches were the first Christian sermons.

40 Days With… The Acts of the Apostles, Vol. 1 begins just after the resurrection, with Jesus still appearing to the Disciples. The story continues with Jesus' ascension up to heaven and the early ministry of the now Apostles. Volume 1 concludes with Paul and Barnabas being chosen by the Holy Spirit for their first missionary journey.

40 Days With… The Acts of the Apostles, Vol. 2 continues with the first missionary journey and follows Paul on his second, third, and fourth missionary journeys. Acts concludes with Paul's arrival in Rome as he waits for his chance to appeal to Caesar.

Also Noteworthy:

In Acts, Luke uses titles for Jesus not found in the Gospels, including 'Holy Servant', 'Author of Life', 'Righteous One', and 'Lord of All'. Comparisons of the Paul found in Acts with the way Paul presents himself in his Epistles are interesting. For example, the Epistles frequently mention a charitable relief fund but this fund is barely mentioned in Acts. In Acts, Paul's states and implies he is a practicing Jew (present tense.) However, in the Epistles, Paul presents his Jewish pedigree as something behind him (past tense.) Also, note how Paul defends himself between audiences of ascending importance. He starts with crowds, then defends himself before the Sanhedrin, then the Roman Governor, then King Herod Agrippa. Acts ends with Paul prepared to defend himself before the Roman Emperor himself.

Devotional Start Date: _____

Day 1	Acts 1:1-5	Key phrase
Key Insight		

Day 2	Acts 1:6-11	Key phrase
Key Insight		

Day 3	Acts 1:12-26	Key phrase
Key Insight		

Day 4	Acts 2:1-13	Key phrase
Key Insight		

Day 5	Acts 2:14-21	Key phrase
Key Insight		

Day 6	Acts 2:22-36	Key phrase

Key Insight

Day 7	Acts 2:37-47	Key phrase

Key Insight

Day 8	Acts 3:1-10	Key phrase

Key Insight

Day 9	Acts 3:11-16	Key phrase

Key Insight

Day 10	Acts 3:17-26	Key phrase

Key Insight

Day 11	Acts 4:1-12	Key phrase

Key Insight

Day 12	Acts 4:13-22	Key phrase

Key Insight

Day 13	Acts 4:23-31	Key phrase

Key Insight

Day 14	Acts 4:32 – 5:11	Key phrase

Key Insight

Day 15	Acts 5:12-16	Key phrase

Key Insight

Day 16	Acts 5:17-26	Key phrase

Key Insight

Day 17	Acts 5:27-42	Key phrase

Key Insight

Day 18	Acts 6:1-15	Key phrase

Key Insight

Day 19	Acts 7:1-16	Key phrase

Key Insight

Day 20	Acts 7:17-22	Key phrase

Key Insight

Day 21	Acts 7:23-34	Key phrase

Key Insight

Day 22	Acts 7:35-43	Key phrase

Key Insight

Day 23	Acts 7:44-53	Key phrase

Key Insight

Day 24	Acts 7:54 – 8:3	Key phrase

Key Insight

Day 25	Acts 8:4-13	Key phrase

Key Insight

Day 26	Acts 8:14-25	Key phrase

Key Insight

Day 27	Acts 8:26-40	Key phrase

Key Insight

Day 28	Acts 9:1-9	Key phrase

Key Insight

Day 29	Acts 9:10-25	Key phrase

Key Insight

Day 30	Acts 9:26-35	Key phrase

Key Insight

Day 31	Acts 9:36-43	Key phrase

Key Insight

Day 32	Acts 10:1-16	Key phrase

Key Insight

Day 33	Acts 10:17-33	Key phrase

Key Insight

Day 34	Acts 10:34-48	Key phrase

Key Insight

Day 35	Acts 11:1-18	Key phrase

Key Insight

Day 36	Acts 11:19-30	Key phrase

Key Insight

Day 37	Acts 12:1-10	Key phrase

Key Insight

Day 38	Acts 12:11-17	Key phrase

Key Insight

Day 39	Acts 12:18-25	Key phrase

Key Insight

Day 40	Acts 13:1-12	Key phrase

Key Insight

ONE FINAL THOUGHT...

If you are familiar with the day's passage, avoid the trap of rushing through it. I believe the Holy Spirit speaks to us through Scripture if we allow the proper time and space. Too often when we encounter a familiar Scripture, we allow our minds to rush to the end ("Oh yeah… I know how that parable ends."). Our minds turn away from Scripture to our normal mental clutter. As you progress through the devotional, avoid this trap and listen carefully to what the Scripture is saying to you today. Try to erase any preconceptions about the passage and approach it with fresh eyes and ears. I have found this practice to be incredibly fruitful in my own personal study. I notice things I never noticed before and I hear things I've missed over and over in prior readings.

Acts 1:1-5

1 Theophilus, the first scroll I wrote concerned everything Jesus did and taught from the beginning, ² right up to the day when he was taken up into heaven. Before he was taken up, working in the power of the Holy Spirit, Jesus instructed the apostles he had chosen.

3 After his suffering, he showed them that he was alive with many convincing proofs. He appeared to them over a period of forty days, speaking to them about God's kingdom.

4 While they were eating together, he ordered them not to leave Jerusalem but to wait for what the Father had promised. He said, "This is what you heard from me:

5 John baptized with water, but in only a few days you will be baptized with the Holy Spirit."

Key words or phrases?

Insights?

Acts 1:6-11

6 As a result, those who had gathered together asked Jesus, "Lord, are you going to restore the kingdom to Israel now?"

7 Jesus replied, "It isn't for you to know the times or seasons that the Father has set by his own authority.

8 Rather, you will receive power when the Holy Spirit has come upon you, and you will be my witnesses in Jerusalem, in all Judea and Samaria, and to the end of the earth."

9 After Jesus said these things, as they were watching, he was lifted up and a cloud took him out of their sight.

10 While he was going away and as they were staring toward heaven, suddenly two men in white robes stood next to them.

11 They said, "Galileans, why are you standing here, looking toward heaven? This Jesus, who was taken up from you into heaven, will come in the same way that you saw him go into heaven."

Key words or phrases?

Insights?

Acts 1:12-26

12   Then they returned to Jerusalem from the Mount of Olives, which is near Jerusalem—a sabbath day's journey away.

13   When they entered the city, they went to the upstairs room where they were staying. Peter, John, James, and Andrew; Philip and Thomas; Bartholomew and Matthew; James, Alphaeus' son; Simon the zealot; and Judas, James' son— ¹⁴ all were united in their devotion to prayer, along with some women, including Mary the mother of Jesus, and his brothers.

15   During this time, the family of believers was a company of about one hundred twenty persons. Peter stood among them and said, ¹⁶ "Brothers and sisters, the scripture that the Holy Spirit announced beforehand through David had to be fulfilled. This was the scripture concerning Judas, who became a guide for those who arrested Jesus.

17   his happened even though he was one of us and received a share of this ministry."

(¹⁸   In fact, he bought a field with the payment he received for his injustice. Falling headfirst, he burst open in the middle and all his intestines spilled out.

19   This became known to everyone living in Jerusalem, so they called that field in their own language Hakeldama, or "Field of Blood.")

20   "It is written in the Psalms scroll,

Let his home become deserted and let there be no one living in it;

and

Give his position of leadership to another.

21 "Therefore, we must select one of those who have accompanied us during the whole time the Lord Jesus lived among us, 22 beginning from the baptism of John until the day when Jesus was taken from us. This person must become along with us a witness to his resurrection."

23 So they nominated two: Joseph called Barsabbas, who was also known as Justus, and Matthias.

24 They prayed, "Lord, you know everyone's deepest thoughts and desires. Show us clearly which one you have chosen from among these two 25 to take the place of this ministry and apostleship, from which Judas turned away to go to his own place."

26 When they cast lots, the lot fell on Matthias. He was added to the eleven apostles.

Key words or phrases?

Insights?

Acts 2:1-13

1   When Pentecost Day arrived, they were all together in one place.

2   Suddenly a sound from heaven like the howling of a fierce wind filled the entire house where they were sitting.

3   They saw what seemed to be individual flames of fire alighting on each one of them.

4   They were all filled with the Holy Spirit and began to speak in other languages as the Spirit enabled them to speak.

5   There were pious Jews from every nation under heaven living in Jerusalem.

6   When they heard this sound, a crowd gathered. They were mystified because everyone heard them speaking in their native languages.

7   They were surprised and amazed, saying, "Look, aren't all the people who are speaking Galileans, every one of them?

8   How then can each of us hear them speaking in our native language?

9   Parthians, Medes, and Elamites; as well as residents of Mesopotamia, Judea, and Cappadocia, Pontus and Asia, 10 Phrygia and Pamphylia, Egypt and the regions of Libya bordering Cyrene; and visitors from Rome (both Jews and converts to Judaism), 11 Cretans and Arabs—we hear them declaring the mighty works of God in our own languages!"

12 They were all surprised and bewildered. Some asked each other, "What does this mean?"

13 Others jeered at them, saying, "They're full of new wine!"

Key words or phrases?

Insights?

Acts 2:14-21

14 Peter stood with the other eleven apostles. He raised his voice and declared, "Judeans and everyone living in Jerusalem! Know this! Listen carefully to my words!

15 These people aren't drunk, as you suspect; after all, it's only nine o'clock in the morning!

16 Rather, this is what was spoken through the prophet Joel:

17 *In the last days, God says,*
I will pour out my Spirit on all people.
Your sons and daughters will prophesy.
Your young will see visions.
Your elders will dream dreams.

18 *Even upon my servants, men and women,*
I will pour out my Spirit in those days,
and they will prophesy.

19 *I will cause wonders to occur in the heavens above*
and signs on the earth below,
blood and fire and a cloud of smoke.

20 *The sun will be changed into darkness,*
and the moon will be changed into blood,
before the great and spectacular day of the Lord comes.

21 *And everyone who calls on the name of the Lord will be*
saved.

Key words or phrases?

Insights?

Acts 2:22-36

²² "Fellow Israelites, listen to these words! Jesus the Nazarene was a man whose credentials God proved to you through miracles, wonders, and signs, which God performed through him among you. You yourselves know this.

²³ In accordance with God's established plan and foreknowledge, he was betrayed. You, with the help of wicked men, had Jesus killed by nailing him to a cross.

²⁴ God raised him up! God freed him from death's dreadful grip, since it was impossible for death to hang on to him.

²⁵ David says about him,

> *I foresaw that the Lord was always with me;*
> *because he is at my right hand I won't be shaken.*

> ²⁶ *Therefore, my heart was glad*
> *and my tongue rejoiced.*
> *Moreover, my body will live in hope,*
> ²⁷ *because you won't abandon me to the grave,*
> *nor permit your holy one to experience decay.*
> ²⁸ *You have shown me the paths of life;*
> *your presence will fill me with happiness.*

²⁹ "Brothers and sisters, I can speak confidently about the patriarch David. He died and was buried, and his tomb is with us to this very day.

³⁰ Because he was a prophet, he knew that God promised him with a solemn pledge to seat one of his descendants on his throne.

31 Having seen this beforehand, David spoke about the resurrection of Christ, that *he wasn't abandoned to the grave, nor did his body experience decay.*

32 This Jesus, God raised up. We are all witnesses to that fact.

33 He was exalted to God's right side and received from the Father the promised Holy Spirit. He poured out this Spirit, and you are seeing and hearing the results of his having done so.

34 David didn't ascend into heaven. Yet he says,

The Lord said to my Lord, 'Sit at my right side,
35   *until I make your enemies a footstool for your feet.'*

36 "Therefore, let all Israel know beyond question that God has made this Jesus, whom you crucified, both Lord and Christ."

Key words or phrases?

Insights?

Acts 2:37-47

37 When the crowd heard this, they were deeply troubled. They said to Peter and the other apostles, "Brothers, what should we do?"

38 Peter replied, "Change your hearts and lives. Each of you must be baptized in the name of Jesus Christ for the forgiveness of your sins. Then you will receive the gift of the Holy Spirit.

39 This promise is for you, your children, and for all who are far away—as many as the Lord our God invites."

40 With many other words he testified to them and encouraged them, saying, "Be saved from this perverse generation."

41 Those who accepted Peter's message were baptized. God brought about three thousand people into the community on that day.

42 The believers devoted themselves to the apostles' teaching, to the community, to their shared meals, and to their prayers.

43 A sense of awe came over everyone. God performed many wonders and signs through the apostles.

44 All the believers were united and shared everything.

45 They would sell pieces of property and possessions and distribute the proceeds to everyone who needed them.

46 Every day, they met together in the temple and ate in their homes. They shared food with gladness and simplicity.

47 They praised God and demonstrated God's goodness to everyone. The Lord added daily to the community those who were being saved.

Key words or phrases?

Insights?

Acts 3:1-10

1 Peter and John were going up to the temple at three o'clock in the afternoon, the established prayer time.

2 Meanwhile, a man crippled since birth was being carried in. Every day, people would place him at the temple gate known as the Beautiful Gate so he could ask for money from those entering the temple.

3 When he saw Peter and John about to enter, he began to ask them for a gift.

4 Peter and John stared at him. Peter said, "Look at us!"

5 So the man gazed at them, expecting to receive something from them.

6 Peter said, "I don't have any money, but I will give you what I do have. In the name of Jesus Christ the Nazarene, rise up and walk!"

7 Then he grasped the man's right hand and raised him up. At once his feet and ankles became strong.

8 Jumping up, he began to walk around. He entered the temple with them, walking, leaping, and praising God.

9 All the people saw him walking and praising God.

10 They recognized him as the same one who used to sit at the temple's Beautiful Gate asking for money. They were filled with amazement and surprise at what had happened to him.

Key words or phrases?

Insights?

Acts 3:11-16

11   While the healed man clung to Peter and John, all the people rushed toward them at Solomon's Porch, completely amazed.

12   Seeing this, Peter addressed the people: "You Israelites, why are you amazed at this? Why are you staring at us as if we made him walk by our own power or piety?

13   The God of Abraham, Isaac, and Jacob—the God of our ancestors—has glorified his servant Jesus. This is the one you handed over and denied in Pilate's presence, even though he had already decided to release him.

14   You rejected the holy and righteous one, and asked that a murderer be released to you instead.

15   You killed the author of life, the very one whom God raised from the dead. We are witnesses of this.

16   His name itself has made this man strong. That is, because of faith in Jesus' name, God has strengthened this man whom you see and know. The faith that comes through Jesus gave him complete health right before your eyes.

Key words or phrases?

Insights?

Acts 3:17-26

17   "Brothers and sisters, I know you acted in ignorance. So did your rulers.

18   But this is how God fulfilled what he foretold through all the prophets: that his Christ would suffer.

19   Change your hearts and lives! Turn back to God so that your sins may be wiped away.

20   Then the Lord will provide a season of relief from the distress of this age and he will send Jesus, whom he handpicked to be your Christ.

21   Jesus must remain in heaven until the restoration of all things, about which God spoke long ago through his holy prophets.

22   Moses said, *The Lord your God will raise up from your own people a prophet like me. Listen to whatever he tells you.*

23   Whoever doesn't listen to that prophet will be totally cut off from the people.

24   All the prophets who spoke—from Samuel forward—announced these days.

25   You are the heirs of the prophets and the covenant that God made with your ancestors when he told Abraham,

> *Through your descendants, all the families on earth will be blessed.*

26   After God raised his servant, he sent him to you first—to bless you by enabling each of you to turn from your evil ways."

Key words or phrases?

Insights?

Acts 4:1-12

1 While Peter and John were speaking to the people, the priests, the captain of the temple guard, and the Sadducees confronted them.

2 They were incensed that the apostles were teaching the people and announcing that the resurrection of the dead was happening because of Jesus.

3 They seized Peter and John and put them in prison until the next day. (It was already evening.)

4 Many who heard the word became believers, and their number grew to about five thousand.

5 The next day the leaders, elders, and legal experts gathered in Jerusalem, 6 along with Annas the high priest, Caiaphas, John, Alexander, and others from the high priest's family.

7 They had Peter and John brought before them and asked, "By what power or in what name did you do this?"

8 Then Peter, inspired by the Holy Spirit, answered, "Leaders of the people and elders, 9 are we being examined today because something good was done for a sick person, a good deed that healed him?

10 If so, then you and all the people of Israel need to know that this man stands healthy before you because of the name of Jesus Christ the Nazarene—whom you crucified but whom God raised from the dead.

11 This Jesus is the stone you builders rejected; he has become the cornerstone!

12 Salvation can be found in no one else. Throughout the whole world, no other name has been given among humans through which we must be saved."

Key words or phrases?

Insights?

Acts 4:13-22

13 The council was caught by surprise by the confidence with which Peter and John spoke. After all, they understood that these apostles were uneducated and inexperienced. They also recognized that they had been followers of Jesus.

14 However, since the healed man was standing with Peter and John before their own eyes, they had no rebuttal.

15 After ordering them to wait outside, the council members began to confer with each other.

16 "What should we do with these men? Everyone living in Jerusalem is aware of the sign performed through them. It's obvious to everyone and we can't deny it.

17 To keep it from spreading further among the people, we need to warn them not to speak to anyone in this name."

18 When they called Peter and John back, they demanded that they stop all speaking and teaching in the name of Jesus.

19 Peter and John responded, "It's up to you to determine whether it's right before God to obey you rather than God.

20 As for us, we can't stop speaking about what we have seen and heard."

21 They threatened them further, then released them. Because of public support for Peter and John, they couldn't find a way to punish them. Everyone was praising God for what had happened, 22 because the man who had experienced this sign of healing was over 40 years old.

Key words or phrases?

Insights?

Acts 4:23-31

23   After their release, Peter and John returned to the brothers and sisters and reported everything the chief priests and elders had said.

24   They listened, then lifted their voices in unison to God, "Master, you are the one who created the heaven, the earth, the sea, and everything in them.

25   You are the one who spoke by the Holy Spirit through our ancestor David, your servant:

Why did the Gentiles rage,
        and the peoples plot in vain?
    26 *The kings of the earth took their stand*
    and the rulers gathered together as one
        against the Lord and against his Christ.

27   Indeed, both Herod and Pontius Pilate, with Gentiles and Israelites, did gather in this city against your holy servant Jesus, whom you anointed.

28   They did what your power and plan had already determined would happen.

29   Now, Lord, take note of their threats and enable your servants to speak your word with complete confidence.

30   Stretch out your hand to bring healing and enable signs and wonders to be performed through the name of Jesus, your holy servant."

31   After they prayed, the place where they were gathered was shaken. They were all filled with the Holy Spirit and began speaking God's word with confidence.

Key words or phrases?

Insights?

Acts 4:32 – 5:11

32 The community of believers was one in heart and mind. None of them would say, "This is mine!" about any of their possessions, but held everything in common.

33 The apostles continued to bear powerful witness to the resurrection of the Lord Jesus, and an abundance of grace was at work among them all.

34 There were no needy persons among them. Those who owned properties or houses would sell them, bring the proceeds from the sales, 35 and place them in the care and under the authority of the apostles. Then it was distributed to anyone who was in need.

36 Joseph, whom the apostles nicknamed Barnabas (that is, "one who encourages"), was a Levite from Cyprus.

37 He owned a field, sold it, brought the money, and placed it in the care and under the authority of the apostles.

1 However, a man named Ananias, along with his wife Sapphira, sold a piece of property.

2 With his wife's knowledge, he withheld some of the proceeds from the sale. He brought the rest and placed it in the care and under the authority of the apostles.

3 Peter asked, "Ananias, how is it that Satan has influenced you to lie to the Holy Spirit by withholding some of the proceeds from the sale of your land?

4   Wasn't that property yours to keep? After you sold it, wasn't the money yours to do with whatever you wanted? What made you think of such a thing? You haven't lied to other people but to God!"

5   When Ananias heard these words, he dropped dead. Everyone who heard this conversation was terrified.

6   Some young men stood up, wrapped up his body, carried him out, and buried him.

7   About three hours later, his wife entered, but she didn't know what had happened to her husband.

8   Peter asked her, "Tell me, did you and your husband receive this price for the field?" She responded, "Yes, that's the amount."

9   He replied, "How could you scheme with each other to challenge the Lord's Spirit? Look! The feet of those who buried your husband are at the door. They will carry you out too."

10 At that very moment, she dropped dead at his feet. When the young men entered and found her dead, they carried her out and buried her with her husband.

11 Trepidation and dread seized the whole church and all who heard what had happened.

Key words or phrases?

Insights?

Acts 5:12-16

12 The apostles performed many signs and wonders among the people. They would come together regularly at Solomon's Porch.

13 No one from outside the church dared to join them, even though the people spoke highly of them.

14 Indeed, more and more believers in the Lord, large numbers of both men and women, were added to the church.

15 As a result, they would even bring the sick out into the main streets and lay them on cots and mats so that at least Peter's shadow could fall on some of them as he passed by.

16 Even large numbers of persons from towns around Jerusalem would gather, bringing the sick and those harassed by unclean spirits. Everyone was healed.

Key words or phrases?

Insights?

Acts 5:17-26

¹⁷ The high priest, together with his allies, the Sadducees, was overcome with jealousy.

¹⁸ They seized the apostles and made a public show of putting them in prison.

¹⁹ An angel from the Lord opened the prison doors during the night and led them out. The angel told them, ²⁰ "Go, take your place in the temple, and tell the people everything about this new life."

²¹ Early in the morning, they went into the temple as they had been told and began to teach. When the high priest and his colleagues gathered, they convened the Jerusalem Council, that is, the full assembly of Israel's elders. They sent word to the prison to have the apostles brought before them.

²² However, the guards didn't find them in the prison. They returned and reported, ²³ "We found the prison locked and well-secured, with guards standing at the doors, but when we opened the doors we found no one inside!"

²⁴ When they received this news, the captain of the temple guard and the chief priests were baffled and wondered what might be happening.

²⁵ Just then, someone arrived and announced, "Look! The people you put in prison are standing in the temple and teaching the people!"

²⁶ Then the captain left with his guards and brought the apostles back. They didn't use force because they were afraid the people would stone them.

Key words or phrases?

Insights?

Acts 5:27-42

27 The apostles were brought before the council where the high priest confronted them: 28 "In no uncertain terms, we demanded that you not teach in this name. And look at you! You have filled Jerusalem with your teaching. And you are determined to hold us responsible for this man's death."

29 Peter and the apostles replied, "We must obey God rather than humans!

30 The God of our ancestors raised Jesus from the dead—whom you killed by hanging him on a tree.

31 God has exalted Jesus to his right side as leader and savior so that he could enable Israel to change its heart and life and to find forgiveness for sins.

32 We are witnesses of such things, as is the Holy Spirit, whom God has given to those who obey him."

33 When the council members heard this, they became furious and wanted to kill the apostles.

34 One council member, a Pharisee and teacher of the Law named Gamaliel, well-respected by all the people, stood up and ordered that the men be taken outside for a few moments.

35 He said, "Fellow Israelites, consider carefully what you intend to do to these people.

36 Some time ago, Theudas appeared, claiming to be somebody, and some four hundred men joined him. After he was killed, all of his followers scattered, and nothing came of that.

37 Afterward, at the time of the census, Judas the Galilean appeared and got some people to follow him in a revolt. He was killed too, and all his followers scattered far and wide.

38 Here's my recommendation in this case: Distance yourselves from these men. Let them go! If their plan or activity is of human origin, it will end in ruin.

39 If it originates with God, you won't be able to stop them. Instead, you would actually find yourselves fighting God!" The council was convinced by his reasoning.

40 After calling the apostles back, they had them beaten. They ordered them not to speak in the name of Jesus, then let them go.

41 The apostles left the council rejoicing because they had been regarded as worthy to suffer disgrace for the sake of the name.

42 Every day they continued to teach and proclaim the good news that Jesus is the Christ, both in the temple and in houses.

Key words or phrases?

Insights?

Acts 6:1-15

1 About that time, while the number of disciples continued to increase, a complaint arose. Greek-speaking disciples accused the Aramaic-speaking disciples because their widows were being overlooked in the daily food service.

2 The Twelve called a meeting of all the disciples and said, "It isn't right for us to set aside proclamation of God's word in order to serve tables.

3 Brothers and sisters, carefully choose seven well-respected men from among you. They must be well-respected and endowed by the Spirit with exceptional wisdom. We will put them in charge of this concern.

4 As for us, we will devote ourselves to prayer and the service of proclaiming the word."

5 This proposal pleased the entire community. They selected Stephen, a man endowed by the Holy Spirit with exceptional faith, Philip, Prochorus, Nicanor, Timon, Parmenas, and Nicolaus from Antioch, a convert to Judaism.

6 The community presented these seven to the apostles, who prayed and laid their hands on them.

7 God's word continued to grow. The number of disciples in Jerusalem increased significantly. Even a large group of priests embraced the faith.

8 Stephen, who stood out among the believers for the way God's grace was at work in his life and for his exceptional endowment with divine power, was doing great wonders and signs among the people.

9   Opposition arose from some who belonged to the so-called Synagogue of Former Slaves. Members from Cyrene, Alexandria, Cilicia, and Asia entered into debate with Stephen.

10 However, they couldn't resist the wisdom the Spirit gave him as he spoke.

11 Then they secretly enticed some people to claim, "We heard him insult Moses and God."

12 They stirred up the people, the elders, and the legal experts. They caught Stephen, dragged him away, and brought him before the Jerusalem Council.

13 Before the council, they presented false witnesses who testified, "This man never stops speaking against this holy place and the Law.

14 In fact, we heard him say that this man Jesus of Nazareth will destroy this place and alter the customary practices Moses gave us."

15 Everyone seated in the council stared at Stephen, and they saw that his face was radiant, just like an angel's.

Key words or phrases?

Insights?

Acts 7:1-16

1   The high priest asked, "Are these accusations true?"

2   Stephen responded, "Brothers and fathers, listen to me. Our glorious God appeared to our ancestor Abraham while he was still in Mesopotamia, before he settled in Haran.

3   God told him, 'Leave your homeland and kin, and go to the land that I will show you.'

4   So Abraham left the land of the Chaldeans and settled in Haran. After Abraham's father died, God had him resettle in this land where you now live.

5   God didn't give him an inheritance here, not even a square foot of land. However, God did promise to give the land as his possession to him and to his descendants, even though Abraham had no child.

6   God put it this way: *His descendants will be strangers in a land that belongs to others, who will enslave them and abuse them for four hundred years.*

7   *And I will condemn the nation they serve as slaves,* God said, *and afterward they will leave that land and serve me in this place.*

8   God gave him the covenant confirmed through circumcision. Accordingly, eight days after Isaac's birth, Abraham circumcised him. Isaac did the same with Jacob, and Jacob with the twelve patriarchs.

⁹ "Because the patriarchs were jealous of Joseph, they sold him into slavery in Egypt. God was with him, however, ¹⁰ and rescued him from all his troubles. The grace and wisdom he gave Joseph were recognized by Pharaoh, king of Egypt, who appointed him ruler over Egypt and over his whole palace.

¹¹ A famine came upon all Egypt and Canaan, and great hardship came with it. Our ancestors had nothing to eat.

¹² When Jacob heard there was grain in Egypt, he sent our ancestors there for the first time.

¹³ During their second visit, Joseph told his brothers who he was, and Pharaoh learned about Joseph's family.

¹⁴ Joseph sent for his father Jacob and all his relatives— seventy-five in all—and invited them to live with him.

¹⁵ So Jacob went down to Egypt, where he and our ancestors died.

¹⁶ Their bodies were brought back to Shechem and placed in the tomb that Abraham had purchased for a certain sum of money from Hamor's children, who lived in Shechem.

Key words or phrases?

Insights?

Acts 7:17-22

17 "When it was time for God to keep the promise he made to Abraham, the number of our people in Egypt had greatly expanded.

18 But then *another king rose to power over Egypt who didn't know anything about Joseph.*

19 He exploited our people and abused our ancestors. He even forced them to abandon their newly born babies so they would die.

20 That's when Moses was born. He was highly favored by God, and for three months his parents cared for him in their home.

21 After he was abandoned, Pharaoh's daughter adopted and cared for him as though he were her own son.

22 Moses learned everything Egyptian wisdom had to offer, and he was a man of powerful words and deeds.

Key words or phrases?

Insights?

Acts 7:23-34

23 "When Moses was 40 years old, he decided to visit his family, the Israelites.

24 He saw one of them being wronged so he came to his rescue and evened the score by killing the Egyptian.

25 He expected his own kin to understand that God was using him to rescue them, but they didn't.

26 The next day he came upon some Israelites who were caught up in an argument. He tried to make peace between them by saying, 'You are brothers! Why are you harming each other?'

27 The one who started the fight against his neighbor pushed Moses aside and said, *'Who appointed you as our leader and judge?*

28 *Are you planning to kill me like you killed that Egyptian yesterday?'*

29 When Moses heard this, he fled to Midian, where he lived as an immigrant and had two sons.

30 "Forty years later, an angel appeared to Moses in the flame of a burning bush in the wilderness near Mount Sinai.

31 Enthralled by the sight, Moses approached to get a closer look and he heard the Lord's voice:

32 *'I am the God of your ancestors, the God of Abraham, Isaac, and Jacob.'* Trembling with fear, Moses didn't dare to investigate any further.

33   The Lord continued, *'Remove the sandals from your feet, for the place where you are standing is holy ground.*

34   *I have clearly seen the oppression my people have experienced in Egypt, and I have heard their groaning. I have come down to rescue them. Come! I am sending you to Egypt.'*

Key words or phrases?

Insights?

Acts 7:35-43

35 "This is the same Moses whom they rejected when they asked, 'Who appointed you as our leader and judge?' This is the Moses whom God sent as leader and deliverer. God did this with the help of the angel who appeared before him in the bush.

36 This man led them out after he performed wonders and signs in Egypt at the Red Sea and for forty years in the wilderness.

37 This is the Moses who told the Israelites, *'God will raise up for you a prophet like me from your own people.'*

38 This is the one who was in the assembly in the wilderness with our ancestors and with the angel who spoke to him on Mount Sinai. He is the one who received life-giving words to give to us.

39 He's also the one whom our ancestors refused to obey. Instead, they pushed him aside and, in their thoughts and desires, returned to Egypt.

40 They told Aaron, *'Make us gods that will lead us. As for this Moses who led us out of Egypt, we don't know what's happened to him!'*

41 That's when they made an idol in the shape of a calf, offered a sacrifice to it, and began to celebrate what they had made with their own hands.

42 So God turned away from them and handed them over to worship the stars in the sky, just as it is written in the scroll of the Prophets:

Did you bring sacrifices and offerings to me
    for forty years in the wilderness, house of Israel?
43 *No! Instead, you took the tent of Moloch with you,*
    and the star of your god Rephan,
    the images that you made in order to worship them.
        Therefore, I will send you far away, farther than
        Babylon.

Key words or phrases?

Insights?

Acts 7:44-53

44 "The tent of testimony was with our ancestors in the wilderness. Moses built it just as he had been instructed by the one who spoke to him and according to the pattern he had seen.

45 In time, when they had received the tent, our ancestors carried it with them when, under Joshua's leadership, they took possession of the land from the nations whom God expelled. This tent remained in the land until the time of David.

46 God approved of David, who asked that he might provide a dwelling place for the God of Jacob.

47 But it was Solomon who actually built a house for God.

48 However, the Most High doesn't live in houses built by human hands. As the prophet says,

49 *Heaven is my throne,*

and the earth is my footstool.

'What kind of house will you build for me,' says the Lord,

'or where is my resting place?

50 *Didn't I make all these things with my own hand?'*

51 "You stubborn people! In your thoughts and hearing, you are like those who have had no part in God's covenant! You continuously set yourself against the Holy Spirit, just like your ancestors did.

52 Was there a single prophet your ancestors didn't harass? They even killed those who predicted the coming of the righteous one, and you've betrayed and murdered him!

53 You received the Law given by angels, but you haven't kept it."

Key words or phrases?

Insights?

Acts 7:54 – 8:3

54 Once the council members heard these words, they were enraged and began to grind their teeth at Stephen.

55 But Stephen, enabled by the Holy Spirit, stared into heaven and saw God's majesty and Jesus standing at God's right side.

56 He exclaimed, "Look! I can see heaven on display and the Human One standing at God's right side!"

57 At this, they shrieked and covered their ears. Together, they charged at him, 58 threw him out of the city, and began to stone him. The witnesses placed their coats in the care of a young man named Saul.

59 As they battered him with stones, Stephen prayed, "Lord Jesus, accept my life!"

60 Falling to his knees, he shouted, "Lord, don't hold this sin against them!" Then he died.

1 Saul was in full agreement with Stephen's murder. At that time, the church in Jerusalem began to be subjected to vicious harassment. Everyone except the apostles was scattered throughout the regions of Judea and Samaria.

2 Some pious men buried Stephen and deeply grieved over him.

3 Saul began to wreak havoc against the church. Entering one house after another, he would drag off both men and women and throw them into prison.

Key words or phrases?

Insights?

Acts 8:4-13

4   Those who had been scattered moved on, preaching the good news along the way.

5   Philip went down to a city in Samaria and began to preach Christ to them.

6   The crowds were united by what they heard Philip say and the signs they saw him perform, and they gave him their undivided attention.

7   With loud shrieks, unclean spirits came out of many people, and many who were paralyzed or crippled were healed.

8   There was great rejoicing in that city.

9   Before Philip's arrival, a certain man named Simon had practiced sorcery in that city and baffled the people of Samaria. He claimed to be a great person.

10 Everyone, from the least to the greatest, gave him their undivided attention and referred to him as "the power of God called Great."

11 He had their attention because he had baffled them with sorcery for a long time.

12 After they came to believe Philip, who preached the good news about God's kingdom and the name of Jesus Christ, both men and women were baptized.

13 Even Simon himself came to believe and was baptized. Afterward, he became one of Philip's supporters. As he saw firsthand the signs and great miracles that were happening, he was astonished.

Key words or phrases?

Insights?

Acts 8:14-25

¹⁴ When word reached the apostles in Jerusalem that Samaria had accepted God's word, they commissioned Peter and John to go to Samaria.

¹⁵ Peter and John went down to Samaria where they prayed that the new believers would receive the Holy Spirit.

(¹⁶ This was because the Holy Spirit had not yet fallen on any of them; they had only been baptized in the name of the Lord Jesus.)

¹⁷ So Peter and John laid their hands on them, and they received the Holy Spirit.

¹⁸ When Simon perceived that the Spirit was given through the laying on of the apostles' hands, he offered them money.

¹⁹ He said, "Give me this authority too so that anyone on whom I lay my hands will receive the Holy Spirit."

²⁰ Peter responded, "May your money be condemned to hell along with you because you believed you could buy God's gift with money!

²¹ You can have no part or share in God's word because your heart isn't right with God.

²² Therefore, change your heart and life! Turn from your wickedness! Plead with the Lord in the hope that your wicked intent can be forgiven, ²³ for I see that your bitterness has poisoned you and evil has you in chains."

24   Simon replied, "All of you, please, plead to the Lord for me so that nothing of what you have said will happen to me!"

25   After the apostles had testified and proclaimed the Lord's word, they returned to Jerusalem, preaching the good news to many Samaritan villages along the way.

Key words or phrases?

Insights?

Acts 8:26-40

26 An angel from the Lord spoke to Philip, "At noon, take the road that leads from Jerusalem to Gaza." (This is a desert road.)

27 So he did. Meanwhile, an Ethiopian man was on his way home from Jerusalem, where he had come to worship. He was a eunuch and an official responsible for the entire treasury of Candace. (Candace is the title given to the Ethiopian queen.)

28 He was reading the prophet Isaiah while sitting in his carriage.

29 The Spirit told Philip, "Approach this carriage and stay with it."

30 Running up to the carriage, Philip heard the man reading the prophet Isaiah. He asked, "Do you really understand what you are reading?"

31 The man replied, "Without someone to guide me, how could I?" Then he invited Philip to climb up and sit with him.

32 This was the passage of scripture he was reading:

> *Like a sheep he was led to the slaughter*
> > *and like a lamb before its shearer is silent*
> > *so he didn't open his mouth.*
> 33 *In his humiliation justice was taken away from him.*
> *Who can tell the story of his descendants*
> > *because his life was taken from the earth?*

34 The eunuch asked Philip, "Tell me, about whom does the prophet say this? Is he talking about himself or someone else?"

35 Starting with that passage, Philip proclaimed the good news about Jesus to him.

36 As they went down the road, they came to some water. The eunuch said, "Look! Water! What would keep me from being baptized?"

38 He ordered that the carriage halt. Both Philip and the eunuch went down to the water, where Philip baptized him.

39 When they came up out of the water, the Lord's Spirit suddenly took Philip away. The eunuch never saw him again but went on his way rejoicing.

40 Philip found himself in Azotus. He traveled through that area, preaching the good news in all the cities until he reached Caesarea.

Key words or phrases?

Insights?

Acts 9:1-9

¹ Meanwhile, Saul was still spewing out murderous threats against the Lord's disciples. He went to the high priest, ² seeking letters to the synagogues in Damascus. If he found persons who belonged to the Way, whether men or women, these letters would authorize him to take them as prisoners to Jerusalem.

³ During the journey, as he approached Damascus, suddenly a light from heaven encircled him.

⁴ He fell to the ground and heard a voice asking him, "Saul, Saul, why are you harassing me?"

⁵ Saul asked, "Who are you, Lord?" "I am Jesus, whom you are harassing," came the reply.

⁶ "Now get up and enter the city. You will be told what you must do."

⁷ Those traveling with him stood there speechless; they heard the voice but saw no one.

⁸ After they picked Saul up from the ground, he opened his eyes but he couldn't see. So they led him by the hand into Damascus.

⁹ For three days he was blind and neither ate nor drank anything.

Key words or phrases?

Insights?

Acts 9:10-25

¹⁰ In Damascus there was a certain disciple named Ananias. The Lord spoke to him in a vision, "Ananias!" He answered, "Yes, Lord."

¹¹ The Lord instructed him, "Go to Judas' house on Straight Street and ask for a man from Tarsus named Saul. He is praying.

¹² In a vision he has seen a man named Ananias enter and put his hands on him to restore his sight."

¹³ Ananias countered, "Lord, I have heard many reports about this man. People say he has done horrible things to your holy people in Jerusalem.

¹⁴ He's here with authority from the chief priests to arrest everyone who calls on your name."

¹⁵ The Lord replied, "Go! This man is the agent I have chosen to carry my name before Gentiles, kings, and Israelites.

¹⁶ I will show him how much he must suffer for the sake of my name."

¹⁷ Ananias went to the house. He placed his hands on Saul and said, "Brother Saul, the Lord sent me—Jesus, who appeared to you on the way as you were coming here. He sent me so that you could see again and be filled with the Holy Spirit."

¹⁸ Instantly, flakes fell from Saul's eyes and he could see again. He got up and was baptized. ¹⁹ After eating, he regained his strength. He stayed with the disciples in Damascus for several days.

20 Right away, he began to preach about Jesus in the synagogues. "He is God's Son," he declared.

21 Everyone who heard him was baffled. They questioned each other, "Isn't he the one who was wreaking havoc among those in Jerusalem who called on this name? Hadn't he come here to take those same people as prisoners to the chief priests?"

22 But Saul grew stronger and stronger. He confused the Jews who lived in Damascus by proving that Jesus is the Christ.

23 After this had gone on for some time, the Jews hatched a plot to kill Saul.

24 However, he found out about their scheme. They were keeping watch at the city gates around the clock so they could assassinate him.

25 But his disciples took him by night and lowered him in a basket through an opening in the city wall.

Key words or phrases?

Insights?

Acts 9:26-35

26 When Saul arrived in Jerusalem, he tried to join the disciples, but they were all afraid of him. They didn't believe he was really a disciple.

27 Then Barnabas brought Saul to the apostles and told them the story about how Saul saw the Lord on the way and that the Lord had spoken to Saul. He also told them about the confidence with which Saul had preached in the name of Jesus in Damascus.

28 After this, Saul moved freely among the disciples in Jerusalem and was speaking with confidence in the name of the Lord.

29 He got into debates with the Greek-speaking Jews as well, but they tried to kill him.

30 When the family of believers learned about this, they escorted him down to Caesarea and sent him off to Tarsus.

31 Then the church throughout Judea, Galilee, and Samaria enjoyed a time of peace. God strengthened the church, and its life was marked by reverence for the Lord. Encouraged by the Holy Spirit, the church continued to grow in numbers.

32 As Peter toured the whole region, he went to visit God's holy people in Lydda.

33 There he found a man named Aeneas who was paralyzed and had been confined to his bed for eight years.

34 Peter said to him, "Aeneas, Jesus Christ heals you! Get up and make your bed." At once he got up.

35 Everyone who lived in Lydda and Sharon saw him and turned to the Lord.

Key words or phrases?

Insights?

Acts 9:36-43

36 In Joppa there was a disciple named Tabitha (in Greek her name is Dorcas). Her life overflowed with good works and compassionate acts on behalf of those in need.

37 About that time, though, she became so ill that she died. After they washed her body, they laid her in an upstairs room.

38 Since Lydda was near Joppa, when the disciples heard that Peter was there, they sent two people to Peter. They urged, "Please come right away!"

39 Peter went with them. Upon his arrival, he was taken to the upstairs room. All the widows stood beside him, crying as they showed the tunics and other clothing Dorcas made when she was alive.

40 Peter sent everyone out of the room, then knelt and prayed. He turned to the body and said, "Tabitha, get up!" She opened her eyes, saw Peter, and sat up.

41 He gave her his hand and raised her up. Then he called God's holy people, including the widows, and presented her alive to them.

42 The news spread throughout Joppa, and many put their faith in the Lord.

43 Peter stayed for some time in Joppa with a certain tanner named Simon.

Key words or phrases?

Insights?

Acts 10:1-16

¹ There was a man in Caesarea named Cornelius, a centurion in the Italian Company.

² He and his whole household were pious, Gentile God-worshippers. He gave generously to those in need among the Jewish people and prayed to God constantly.

³ One day at nearly three o'clock in the afternoon, he clearly saw an angel from God in a vision. The angel came to him and said, "Cornelius!"

⁴ Startled, he stared at the angel and replied, "What is it, Lord?" The angel said, "Your prayers and your compassionate acts are like a memorial offering to God.

⁵ Send messengers to Joppa at once and summon a certain Simon, the one known as Peter.

⁶ He is a guest of Simon the tanner, whose house is near the seacoast."

⁷ When the angel who was speaking to him had gone, Cornelius summoned two of his household servants along with a pious soldier from his personal staff.

⁸ He explained everything to them, then sent them to Joppa.

⁹ At noon on the following day, as their journey brought them close to the city, Peter went up on the roof to pray.

¹⁰ He became hungry and wanted to eat. While others were preparing the meal, he had a visionary experience.

11 He saw heaven opened up and something like a large linen sheet being lowered to the earth by its four corners.

12 Inside the sheet were all kinds of four-legged animals, reptiles, and wild birds.

13 A voice told him, "Get up, Peter! Kill and eat!"

14 Peter exclaimed, "Absolutely not, Lord! I have never eaten anything impure or unclean."

15 The voice spoke a second time, "Never consider unclean what God has made pure."

16 This happened three times, then the object was suddenly pulled back into heaven.

Key words or phrases?

Insights?

Acts 10:17-33

¹⁷ Peter was bewildered about the meaning of the vision. Just then, the messengers sent by Cornelius discovered the whereabouts of Simon's house and arrived at the gate.

¹⁸ Calling out, they inquired whether the Simon known as Peter was a guest there.

¹⁹ While Peter was brooding over the vision, the Spirit interrupted him, "Look! Three people are looking for you.

²⁰ Go downstairs. Don't ask questions; just go with them because I have sent them."

²¹ So Peter went downstairs and told them, "I'm the one you are looking for. Why have you come?"

²² They replied, "We've come on behalf of Cornelius, a centurion and righteous man, a God-worshipper who is well-respected by all Jewish people. A holy angel directed him to summon you to his house and to hear what you have to say."

²³ Peter invited them into the house as his guests. The next day he got up and went with them, together with some of the believers from Joppa.

²⁴ They arrived in Caesarea the following day. Anticipating their arrival, Cornelius had gathered his relatives and close friends.

²⁵ As Peter entered the house, Cornelius met him and fell at his feet in order to honor him.

²⁶ But Peter lifted him up, saying, "Get up! Like you, I'm just a human."

27 As they continued to talk, Peter went inside and found a large gathering of people.

28 He said to them, "You all realize that it is forbidden for a Jew to associate or visit with outsiders. However, God has shown me that I should never call a person impure or unclean.

29 For this reason, when you sent for me, I came without objection. I want to know, then, why you sent for me."

30 Cornelius answered, "Four days ago at this same time, three o'clock in the afternoon, I was praying at home. Suddenly a man in radiant clothing stood before me.

31 He said, 'Cornelius, God has heard your prayers, and your compassionate acts are like a memorial offering to him.

32 Therefore, send someone to Joppa and summon Simon, who is known as Peter. He is a guest in the home of Simon the tanner, located near the seacoast.'

33 I sent for you right away, and you were kind enough to come. Now, here we are, gathered in the presence of God to listen to everything the Lord has directed you to say."

Key words or phrases?

Insights?

Acts 10:34-48

34 Peter said, "I really am learning that God doesn't show partiality to one group of people over another.

35 Rather, in every nation, whoever worships him and does what is right is acceptable to him.

36 This is the message of peace he sent to the Israelites by proclaiming the good news through Jesus Christ: He is Lord of all!

37 You know what happened throughout Judea, beginning in Galilee after the baptism John preached.

38 You know about Jesus of Nazareth, whom God anointed with the Holy Spirit and endowed with power. Jesus traveled around doing good and healing everyone oppressed by the devil because God was with him.

39 We are witnesses of everything he did, both in Judea and in Jerusalem. They killed him by hanging him on a tree, 40 but God raised him up on the third day and allowed him to be seen, 41 not by everyone but by us. We are witnesses whom God chose beforehand, who ate and drank with him after God raised him from the dead.

42 He commanded us to preach to the people and to testify that he is the one whom God appointed as judge of the living and the dead.

43 All the prophets testify about him that everyone who believes in him receives forgiveness of sins through his name."

44 While Peter was still speaking, the Holy Spirit fell on everyone who heard the word.

45 The circumcised believers who had come with Peter were astonished that the gift of the Holy Spirit had been poured out even on the Gentiles.

46 They heard them speaking in other languages and praising God. Peter asked, 47 "These people have received the Holy Spirit just as we have. Surely no one can stop them from being baptized with water, can they?"

48 He directed that they be baptized in the name of Jesus Christ. Then they invited Peter to stay for several days.

Key words or phrases?

Insights?

Acts 11:1-18

1 The apostles and the brothers and sisters throughout Judea heard that even the Gentiles had welcomed God's word.

2 When Peter went up to Jerusalem, the circumcised believers criticized him.

3 They accused him, "You went into the home of the uncircumcised and ate with them!"

4 Step-by-step, Peter explained what had happened.

5 "I was in the city of Joppa praying when I had a visionary experience. In my vision, I saw something like a large linen sheet being lowered from heaven by its four corners. It came all the way down to me.

6 As I stared at it, wondering what it was, I saw four-legged animals—including wild beasts—as well as reptiles and wild birds.

7 I heard a voice say, 'Get up, Peter! Kill and eat!'

8 I responded, 'Absolutely not, Lord! Nothing impure or unclean has ever entered my mouth.'

9 The voice from heaven spoke a second time, 'Never consider unclean what God has made pure.'

10 This happened three times, then everything was pulled back into heaven.

11 At that moment three men who had been sent to me from Caesarea arrived at the house where we were staying.

12 The Spirit told me to go with them even though they were Gentiles. These six brothers also went with me, and we entered that man's house.

13 He reported to us how he had seen an angel standing in his house and saying, 'Send to Joppa and summon Simon, who is known as Peter.

14 He will tell you how you and your entire household can be saved.'

15 When I began to speak, the Holy Spirit fell on them, just as the Spirit fell on us in the beginning.

16 I remembered the Lord's words: 'John will baptize with water, but you will be baptized with the Holy Spirit.'

17 If God gave them the same gift he gave us who believed in the Lord Jesus Christ, then who am I? Could I stand in God's way?"

18 Once the apostles and other believers heard this, they calmed down. They praised God and concluded, "So then God has enabled Gentiles to change their hearts and lives so that they might have new life."

Key words or phrases?

Insights?

Acts 11:19-30

¹⁹ Now those who were scattered as a result of the trouble that occurred because of Stephen traveled as far as Phoenicia, Cyprus, and Antioch. They proclaimed the word only to Jews.

²⁰ Among them were some people from Cyprus and Cyrene. They entered Antioch and began to proclaim the good news about the Lord Jesus also to Gentiles.

²¹ The Lord's power was with them, and a large number came to believe and turned to the Lord.

²² When the church in Jerusalem heard about this, they sent Barnabas to Antioch.

²³ When he arrived and saw evidence of God's grace, he was overjoyed and encouraged everyone to remain fully committed to the Lord.

²⁴ Barnabas responded in this way because he was a good man, whom the Holy Spirit had endowed with exceptional faith. A considerable number of people were added to the Lord.

²⁵ Barnabas went to Tarsus in search of Saul.

²⁶ When he found him, he brought him to Antioch. They were there for a whole year, meeting with the church and teaching large numbers of people. It was in Antioch where the disciples were first labeled "Christians."

²⁷ About that time, some prophets came down from Jerusalem to Antioch.

28   One of them, Agabus, stood up and, inspired by the Spirit, predicted that a severe famine would overtake the entire Roman world. (This occurred during Claudius' rule.)

29   The disciples decided they would send support to the brothers and sisters in Judea, with everyone contributing to this ministry according to each person's abundance.

30   They sent Barnabas and Saul to take this gift to the elders.

Key words or phrases?

Insights?

Acts 12:1-10

1 About that time King Herod began to harass some who belonged to the church.

2 He had James, John's brother, killed with a sword.

3 When he saw that this pleased the Jews, he arrested Peter as well. This happened during the Festival of Unleavened Bread.

4 He put Peter in prison, handing him over to four squads of soldiers, sixteen in all, who guarded him. He planned to charge him publicly after the Passover.

5 While Peter was held in prison, the church offered earnest prayer to God for him.

6 The night before Herod was going to bring Peter's case forward, Peter was asleep between two soldiers and bound with two chains, with soldiers guarding the prison entrance.

7 Suddenly an angel from the Lord appeared and a light shone in the prison cell. After nudging Peter on his side to awaken him, the angel raised him up and said, "Quick! Get up!" The chains fell from his wrists.

8 The angel continued, "Get dressed. Put on your sandals." Peter did as he was told. The angel said, "Put on your coat and follow me."

9 Following the angel, Peter left the prison. However, he didn't realize the angel had actually done all this. He thought he was seeing a vision.

10 They passed the first and second guards and came to the iron gate leading to the city. It opened for them by itself. After leaving the prison, they proceeded the length of one street, when abruptly the angel was gone.

Key words or phrases?

Insights?

Acts 12:11-17

11 At that, Peter came to his senses and remarked, "Now I'm certain that the Lord sent his angel and rescued me from Herod and from everything the Jewish people expected."

12 Realizing this, he made his way to Mary's house. (Mary was John's mother; he was also known as Mark.) Many believers had gathered there and were praying.

13 When Peter knocked at the outer gate, a female servant named Rhoda went to answer.

14 She was so overcome with joy when she recognized Peter's voice that she didn't open the gate. Instead, she ran back in and announced that Peter was standing at the gate.

15 "You've lost your mind!" they responded. She stuck by her story with such determination that they began to say, "It must be his guardian angel."

16 Meanwhile, Peter remained outside, knocking at the gate. They finally opened the gate and saw him there, and they were astounded.

17 He gestured with his hand to quiet them down, then recounted how the Lord led him out of prison. He said, "Tell this to James and the brothers and sisters." Then he left for another place.

Key words or phrases?

Insights?

Acts 12:18-25

18 The next morning the soldiers were flustered about what had happened to Peter.

19 Herod called for a thorough search. When Peter didn't turn up, Herod interrogated the guards and had them executed. Afterward, Herod left Judea in order to spend some time in Caesarea.

20 Herod had been furious with the people of Tyre and Sidon for some time. They made a pact to approach him together, since their region depended on the king's realm for its food supply. They persuaded Blastus, the king's personal attendant, to join their cause, then appealed for an end to hostilities.

21 On the scheduled day Herod dressed himself in royal attire, seated himself on the throne, and gave a speech to the people.

22 Those assembled kept shouting, over and over, "This is a god's voice, not the voice of a mere human!"

23 Immediately an angel from the Lord struck Herod down, because he didn't give the honor to God. He was eaten by worms and died.

24 God's word continued to grow and increase.

25 Barnabas and Saul returned to Antioch from Jerusalem after completing their mission, bringing with them John, who was also known as Mark.

Key words or phrases?

Insights?

Acts 13:1-12

¹ The church at Antioch included prophets and teachers: Barnabas, Simeon (nicknamed Niger), Lucius from Cyrene, Manaen (a childhood friend of Herod the ruler), and Saul.

² As they were worshipping the Lord and fasting, the Holy Spirit said, "Appoint Barnabas and Saul to the work I have called them to undertake."

³ After they fasted and prayed, they laid their hands on these two and sent them off.

⁴ After the Holy Spirit sent them on their way, they went down to Seleucia. From there they sailed to Cyprus.

⁵ In Salamis they proclaimed God's word in the Jewish synagogues. John was with them as their assistant.

⁶ They traveled throughout the island until they arrived at Paphos. There they found a certain man named Bar-Jesus, a Jew who was a false prophet and practiced sorcery.

⁷ He kept company with the governor of that province, an intelligent man named Sergius Paulus. The governor sent for Barnabas and Saul since he wanted to hear God's word.

⁸ But Elymas the sorcerer (for that's what people understood his name meant) opposed them, trying to steer the governor away from the faith.

⁹ Empowered by the Holy Spirit, Saul, also known as Paul, glared at Bar-Jesus and ¹⁰ said, "You are a deceiver and trickster! You devil! You attack anything that is right! Will you never stop twisting the straight ways of the Lord into crooked paths?

11 Listen! The Lord's power is set against you. You will be blind
    for a while, unable even to see the daylight." At once, Bar-Jesus'
    eyes were darkened, and he began to grope about for someone
    to lead him around by the hand.

12 When the governor saw what had taken place, he came to
    believe, for he was astonished by the teaching about the Lord.

Key words or phrases?

Insights?

95879567R00083

Made in the USA
Columbia, SC
23 May 2018